Forever in my Heart

Poems of my Youth

Joe Tallarigo

Thanks for the support

Joe Tally

1

A Word from the Author

These poems are a reflection of my life from 1999 through 2008.

When I was going in as a Freshmen at Oak Hills in September of 1999, I only knew one person, out of the 3,000 students who were going to be my classmates.

My parents suggested I attend Camp Oak Hills in August of 1999,which is a two-day camp at the high school where junior and seniors show the freshmen around the school, build leadership skills, and make new friends. During those two days, I made a few new friends, and became acquainted with the juniors and seniors, and one of the counselors was announced as the Homecoming Queen that October.

On September 7th, I along with 750 plus freshmen were the first freshmen class to roam the hallowed halls in almost 40 years.
The opening of the school day began with a pep rally, and never before had I witnessed a school beginning with such a celebration.

My homeroom ironically was the music room and my homeroom teacher was Mr. Welsh who was the band director.
Through the first few months of homeroom I became the class clown, and made many great friends who helped inspire and guide me through the four years I was there.

The football season was historical, and there was a lot of pride as the football team made it into the state playoffs for the first time ever in school history. Unfortunately they lost the first playoff game. But those few weeks at school were one of excitement.

My first Homecoming dance was in October, and my first dance was with a senior and the song we danced to was Journey's "Faithfully."

By December I began taking a camera to school, and taking pictures of my friends, and soon I got the nickname "Photo Joe" for taking a lot of pictures at school.

In my Junior year of high school in October I wrote my first poem "Stay Around." The words came to me when I was leaving lunch and heading back to my geometry class. I quickly got back to the classroom, took out a piece of paper, wrote the words down, but got stuck on the second verse, so I waited until I got home and wrote the rest of the poem that night.
All in all I wrote around forty poems by the time I graduated Oak Hills in 2003.

After high school, I took some time off, I wasn't going to college, and in September of 2003, my mom's friend called me up saying I should apply to a daycare where her daughter was working at.
So I went up and that began my career in daycares. I worked in daycares from 2003 through 2009 and I got to work twice with my mom at two of the daycares.

In the Fall of 2004, I attended some football games with my brother and cousin since they were graduating the following spring, this was their last games as students, and I wanted to hang out with them since we began going to football games together when I was a freshman in 1999.

The first game I went to was on October 1st, and I was overcoming a lengthy illness, but the weather was warm, and I was regaining my strength, and I was determined to go to the game.

I arrived at the stadium, walked to the student section and climbed the metal stands to where my brother and cousin were sitting, next to the band. As I got to the last metal stand of where they were sitting, I noticed a girl sitting behind my brother and cousin, and instantly I felt something good was going to come of this.

The first half of the game I was feeling a lot better than I had those past few weeks, so at half time I bought my brother, cousin, and his friends two large pizzas.

After the game, I talked to the girl and over the next few weeks all of us had a good time at the football games.

That November I realized I had a lot of fun at the football games, and that's how the first chapter was born. I realized how much fun I had in high school, and at the time I was listening to Country music singer Kenny Chesney who was singing about his life, so I began writing songs about my time in high school, but made them so that anyone could relate to the songs.

The second chapter of my book is titled I-75 to Bowling Green/ Coming Home and is about my time spent in Bowling Green, Ohio where my brother went to college. And to my surprise another special person went there.

I fell in love with the little town, and it helped inspire some songs and made many great memories up there.

The third chapter takes place solely in 2008, when my aunt passed away from cancer at the young age of 51. She was my confidant, and we talk about the Reds, music, the singers at Taste of Cincinnati, Bengals, and she loved Jimmy Buffett who I now listen to a lot. When she passed away my world turned upside down.

Around the same time of my aunt's passing I met another family who became my second family and brought me back to church and God.

Acknowledgements

I dedicate this book to the wonderful teachers and staff at Oak Hills. They are very supportive and caring and want the best for each student who are enrolled there.

I want to give a big shout out to every student who ever attended Oak Hills and who has generations of family attending Oak Hills.

But I want to give the biggest thanks to the classes of 1999 to 2005, and the many great students I met and who inspired me and supported me through the years. We had a lot of fun times and made many great memories. I hope all your dreams and goals come true.

****

If you are a current or future student in high school know that the next four years will fly by fast. I would encourage you to go to the football games, go to the school dances, try out for school plays, and sports. Also don't be afraid to speak your dreams and goals to your friends and teachers. You may find they may be your biggest supporters and will help you grow as a person and help you achieve your dreams and goals.

First Chapter

The Last Quarter
Songs of High School

1999-2003

Highlander Country

We have Westside pride of red and black
our friends have our backs
no matter what we need
we're right on track

We hang out at Fifth and Vine
between classes teachers come out and say hi
to the students walking by
at lunch we'd steal our friends' fries

We're Highlanders
we cheer on our sports teams
the band marches in city parades
we have the best of Oak Hills
where students sing, tell jokes, put on skits
there's nothing in life that's better
and we'll always be Highlanders

We decorate the halls for homecoming
walk with our friends to class
practice our lines for school plays
and take our dates to the dances

We're Highlanders
we cheer on our sports teams
the band marches in city parades
we have the best of Oak Hills
where students sing, tell jokes, put on skits
there's nothing in life that's better
and we'll always be Highlanders

In homeroom I was the class clown
wrote my songs in study hall
got my nickname "Photo Joe"
taking pictures of my friends
to this day I visit my old stomping grounds
one day I'll make them proud.

Oak Hills High School 1959

Ode to Friday Nights

From August to October we'd gather out
in the school parking lots
we'd grill hamburgers and hotdogs
toss a frisbee or play cornhole
sit on the hood of our cars
just to pass the time
on those Friday nights

When they opened up the gates
we were the first in line
to take our seats in the stands
right next to the band
we'd high five each other
as the game got underway

Hot Chocolate and pizza warmed us up
when it got cold out
there was always time
to talk to our friends
sometimes we'd wished
the games would never end

After the game, we would drive
to our favorite hangout, Skyline
we'd order root beer and coneys
on those Friday nights.

The Last Quarter

Twelve minutes to go
my heart is beating fast
my hands are shaking
the band is playing
the crowd is cheering
I wish we were winning
and my head is spinning

Should I ask her, should I not
this last quarter is all I got
if I don't ask her now
then I won't have another chance
to ask her to the Homecoming dance

Five minutes to go
she looks over smiles and waves
our team just made a great play
what should I say

Should I ask her, should I not
this last quarter is all I got
if I don't ask her now
then I won't have another chance
to ask her to the Homecoming dance

Two-minute warning
the game is over, I take her aside
ready to ask her to the dance
but all I say is "good game"
and walk away.

Homecoming

Tuxedoes and pretty dresses
chicken dinner over our cousin's house
getting our photos taken with our dates
in front of their fireplace

We put the tickets into our wallets
then get into the limo
we give our parents
a smile, a wave goodbye
as we pull away

Doors open at eight
lay your purses on the table
hand in hand, we make our way to the dance floor
as the DJ plays "Cotton Eye Joe"

"Amazed" is our first slow dance of the night
don't be timid and shy
place your hand on my shoulders
let the music take us round and round
as we gaze into each other's eyes

Our Homecoming King and Queen
sure look like royalty
everyone claps as their announced and crowned
"Faithfully" is their song and dance
you and I dance slowly, knowing the night is almost over

We meet up with our friends at midnight
take a ride back to our cousin's house
we eat, drink, and talk about
how we had the time of our lives.

More than Friends

Every night when I say my prayers
I ask God to give me the words
to let you know I find it frustrating
that good friends like us
can't seem to fall in love

There's no denying
there's something between us
I enjoy eating lunch together
stealing glances during class
reading the notes you leave in my locker
watching your softball practices and games
working on our homework together
and watching Tv
so tell me

How come good friends like us
can't seem to fall in love
why can't we see
what everyone else sees
they say we make the cutest couple
and I have to agree
so why can't my heart bend and give in
to let you know
I want to be more than friends

Is love supposed to be this hard
or is that we're young
focusing on school, driving tests
trying to get a job
I just pray that one day
we're more than friends.

Road Trip Summer

We have a cooler of pop, bag of snacks
our favorite songs playing on the radio
our suitcases are packed
we're ready to hit the open road

In our road trip summer
we're going coast to coast
first to Boston to see the Red Sox play
then New York City to hang out in Time Square
followed by Myrtle Beach and Panama City
to get the pretty girl's numbers
in our road trip summer

Now we're heading northwest
through the Smokies and Gatlinburg
then we're headed to the top of the Saint Louis Arch
then tickle the ivy at Wrigley Field
drive past the cornfields in Iowa
do some shopping at the Mall of America
then fish in the Land of a Thousand Lakes

In our road trip summer
we're going coast to coast
next up is Seattle to see if it rains everyday
then south to see the Giants and Athletics play
drive on the Golden Gate Bridge
then it's off to L.A.
to Hollywood and the Walk of Fame
and get the pretty girl's numbers
in our road trip summer

No rules, no parents, no teachers
just our friends, white lines, and sunshine
ordering off the dollar menu's, staying in cold motel rooms
buying souvenir t-shirts
in our road trip summer.

One Last Slow Dance

This song is our last slow dance of our high school years
when this song ends it'll be time to go home and go to bed
soon it'll just be another memory
but when I look back on it
I'll be glad I got to share the last slow dance with you

This song is slow
unlike the years that flew by
I never told you
how much you mean to me
I guess it doesn't matter now
now that I have this chance
to share this last slow dance with you

DJ, DJ, please play one more song
it's not yet midnight
this is our first dance of the night
just one more song, just one more dance

Lights turn on this is it
no more songs
so I escort you to your car
and have one more slow dance
beneath the stars.

Long Summer

I woke up this morning with the sun on my face
with last night ceremonies still fresh in my mind
I feel out of place, just lying here in bed
thinking about how I'll miss my friends

It's going to be a long summer
what a bummer when September comes around
and you'll be in a different college town
it's not going to be the same
I'm going to miss walking with you in the hallways
sitting next to you in class
and having our inside jokes
It's going to be a long summer

I look at our pictures when we were freshmen
I laugh now how we thought we'd never fit in
but we made a lot of new friends
we ruled the school
now all we have is scrapbooks
full of memories and good lucks

It's going to be a long summer
what a bummer when September comes around
and you'll be in a different college town
it's not going to be the same
I'm going to miss walking with you in the hallways
sitting next to you in class
and having our inside jokes
It's going to be a long summer

2003 Graduation Ceremony

On the Flipside

We were the best of friends
writing and practicing our songs in our parent's garage
then we would perform them at talent shows and parties
we dreamt of being the next Lennon and McCartney
but time and college drifted us apart

See you on the flipside
where we'll meet again
and pick up where we left off
the spotlight will shine on us
we'll be doing what we love
what we should have done all this time
see you on the flipside

She was the prettiest girl in school
I was the lucky one she wore my class ring
our classmates voted us Prom King and Queen
everyone thought we'd get married
but time and college drifted us apart

See you on the flipside
where we'll meet again
and pick up where we left off
the spotlight will shine on us
we'll be doing what we love
what we should have done all this time
see you on the flipside.

Chapter Two

I-75 to Bowling Green/ Coming Home

2004-2008

September

Leaves aren't the only thing changing this September
I'm packing my clothes, books, and computer
it'll be my first time on my own
soon I'll be moving into my dorm
meeting new friends and learning new things

I remember when September was jumping in leaves
rooting on your favorite football team
telling vacation stories to anyone who'll listen
September was the month to recover
from the hot days of summer
leaves aren't the only thing changing this September

I'm spending these last few August days with my friends
helping them pack, and hanging out at our local haunts
having one last good time
making one last memory
before we go our separate ways

I remember when September was jumping in leaves
rooting on your favorite football team
telling vacation stories to anyone who'll listen
September was the month to recover
from the hot days of summer
leaves aren't the only thing changing this September.

Slow Dancing in the Rain

We were sitting in the lawn seats
waiting for the concert to begin
when those dark clouds opened up
and sent a summer storm upon us

We could have ran for cover
but it felt good on that hot August night
we huddled close together then we began swaying
to the beat of the thunder
everyone looked at us like we were crazy
as we slowed danced in the rain

All through his songs we sang along
as the rain continued to fall
but we didn't mind at all
because we were sharing the night
with our favorite star

We could have ran for cover
but it felt good on that hot August night
we huddled close together then we began swaying
to the beat of the thunder
everyone looked at us like we were crazy
as we slowed danced in the rain

When the concert ended
the dark clouds moved out
for an encore, the stars and moon
lit up that August night for me and you.

No Sad Song for You

There's no sad song for you
none could be written
it wouldn't be true
you always made me smile
made our time together worthwhile
I don't think there's a sad song for you

I never cried over you
though my heart longs for you
I know we may never get together
I just hope we stay friends forever
the songs on the radio they play
don't make me blue

Because there's no sad song for you
none could be written
it wouldn't be true
you always made me smile
made our time together worthwhile
I don't think there's a sad song for you

If one ever did come along
we both would have to write it
because it would be the day
we say goodbye forever
but for now
there's no sad song for you and me.

Cincinnati has been Good to Me

Never thought it be so hard to leave
the only city I ever knew
but we all have to do
what we need to do
it's not going to be easy
since Cincinnati has been good to me

I'll miss Skyline three-ways
Cincinnati Reds games
the concerts down at the Taste
but it's time I chase my dreams
though it's so hard to leave
since Cincinnati has been good to me

I know no one gets where they're going
by wishing upon stars
you have to work hard
to get where you want to be
though sometimes we need a push
to get our wheels turning
but I'll always keep a fire burning for Cincinnati

I'll miss Skyline three-ways
Cincinnati Reds games
the concerts down at the Taste
but it's time I chase my dreams
though it's so hard to leave
since Cincinnati has been good to me.

I-75 to Bowling Green, Ohio

I'm going to get away tonight
I hop onto I-75 to Bowling Green, Ohio
I need to let my mind unwind
it's been forever since I had some downtime

I throw my arms up for Touchdown Jesus in Monroe
that's my cousin's favorite joke
but it's a lonely three-hour drive
passing by Dayton, Piqua, Tipp City, and Findlay
nothing but small towns, and the radio
to keep you company
on I-75 to Bowling Green, Ohio

I'm going to get away tonight
I hop onto I-75 to Bowling Green, Ohio
I need to let my mind unwind
it's been forever since I had some downtime

I feel my troubles fade away
glancing at the open fields
I'm getting closer to exit 181
for a weekend of fun
hanging out with my brother and his friends

I'm going to get away tonight
I hop onto I-75 to Bowling Green, Ohio
I need to let my mind unwind
it's been forever since I had some downtime.

Second Chances

Never would I have guessed
I'd be here sitting next to you
after all we went through
but I guess there was something left
when I asked you out again

Are you being nice
are you just lonely tonight
or are you sincere
are we falling back in love
or is it all the above
these questions I must ask
for our second chance

Don't get me wrong I want your company
there's no place I'd rather be
it's nice to rekindle the old days
and feel the flame I held for you
but can it be true

Are you being nice
are you just lonely tonight
or are you sincere
are we falling back in love
or is it all the above
these questions I must ask
for our second chance.

In my Group of Friends

In my group of friends
we have happy, crazy
hard working people
we like to have fun
in our own twisted ways

In my group of friends
we have a Juggalo, cowboy, DJ
artists, band groupies, good hearted people
who love to have a good time
and make a scene in public
living life like it's one big movie

We like to hang out
stay up late at night
it's alright
if we make fools out of ourselves
we're going to have fun
have our piece of the sun

In my group of friends
we have lovers, brothers,
cousins, long time buddies
it's kind of funny
all the stories we could tell
of our great glories
you'll see our pictures
in our books.

All Night Conversations

Playing video games at two A.M.
with my brother and friends
telling stories of our misspent youth
how we scared ourselves silly
spending the night at each other's houses
we're all laughing, having a good time
getting that natural high
that comes from staying up all night

We talk about our future plans
and what we've been up to
and how boring our lives would be
if we never met
we talk about our women
our past regrets
I don't care telling them what's on my mind
it's all night conversation time

Remember walking to your house after school
trading baseball cards, playing Pokémon card games
reading Goosebumps books
recording yourselves doing crazy stunts
doing all you could to get a laugh
we sure had a lot of good times
and it's fun reliving it all again tonight

Anywhere, anytime, I don't mind who it's with
I love these long nights
when we goof off and unwind
getting a natural high
it's all night conversation time.

My Second Home

Bowling Green, Ohio you're my second home
I never felt such a strong connection
to another town
until I got off at exit 181
when I visited my brother
there's something about your Main Street
with the restaurants, hotels, and campus
all in walking distance of each other

Every Fall and Spring
their Habitat for Humanity
held a contest called box city
for one night my brother, cousins, friends, and I
built and slept in trailers, pirate ships, and castles
that we built out of cardboard boxes

The coffee shop is full of coeds
studying for their classes
there's a record store with a 1970's feel
and one night at midnight we went to the windmills
that sit in the middle of the cornfields

I started to watch "The Office"
began listening to Merle Haggard up there
it didn't hurt the girl I liked went there
and their school colors remind me of a crisp fall day
I can honestly say

Bowling Green, Ohio you're my second home
I never felt such a strong connection
to another town
until I got off at exit 181
when I visited my brother
there's something about your Main Street
with the restaurants, hotels, and campus
all in walking distance of each other.

Nashville Bound

I wish I was in Nashville
like I'd said I'd be when I graduated from high school
but I got jobs at daycares
teaching kids their shapes, letters, and numbers
as they slept during nap time
I'd pull out a pen and paper
to write my songs
wishing I was Nashville bound

In December of 2004
my mom and I attended a songwriter's round
I got an inside view of what I wanted to do
I got to meet each song writer
they gave me advice and told me to keep writing
being there I wanted to be Nashville bound

Every May I'd go down to Country Music concerts at the Taste
wait by the singer's buses
and hoping to get to meet the singers
then I'd watch religiously as they played their songs
being there I wanted to be Nashville bound

In 2005, I broke down and bought a guitar
Johnny A taught me chords and how to play some songs
I got blisters determined to make my way
to the town of my dreams
but I ended up spending a lot of my time in Bowling Green, Ohio
wishing I Nashville bound.

Brush of Love
(Mrs. Kappa's Song)

Piece by piece put together
makes a beautiful masterpiece
colored by your zest for life
in reds, blues, and yellows
then life handed you some troubles

When those days came
your hand painted a scene
from your memories

Be set free, with your wings
fly to Heaven above
color the sky
with your brush of love

Your love for the arts
made our lives brighter
there was a sparkle in your eyes
when your visions were created
decorating the hallways
in mosaics of your life and dreams

Piece by piece it all came together
you colored our lives
with hope and inspiration

Be set free, with your wings
fly to Heaven above
color the sky
with your brush of love.

Mrs. Kappa
Art 4 teacher Oak Hills High School

Rounding Third and Headed for Home (Joe Nuxhall Tribute)

Tonight, in Cincinnati, down by the Ohio River
the stadium lights have gone out
to honor a hometown legend
who's been a big part of our lives
for over sixty years
now it's time to say goodbye
because he rounded home and headed for home

Every Spring and Summer
He brought families together
as they listened to him call the games on the radio
in their homes, cars, or backyards
sometimes we stayed up late
just to listen to Him before we fell asleep

Tonight, in Cincinnati, down by the Ohio River
the stadium lights have gone out
to honor a hometown legend
who's been a big part of our lives
for over sixty years
now it's time to say goodbye
because he rounded home and headed for home

We now miss Him calling the Reds games
The Springs and Summers
aren't the same anymore
since he rounded third and headed for home.

Coming Home

Bring out the yearbooks, bring out the photos
bring back the good times and laughter
I promise I'd be back in a few years
to sing the songs I wrote years ago

Tonight, as I stand on this stage
I see familiar faces in the stands
my dream was to sing my songs
underneath the stadium lights
in front of my friends and teachers
who believed in me all those years ago
now here I am coming home

Things sure have changed since 2003
some friends and teachers have passed away
I've made connections in Nashville
had good times in Bowling Green
but my heart remained in Cincinnati

Tonight, as I stand on this stage
I see familiar faces in the stands
my dream was to sing my songs
underneath the stadium lights
in front of my friends and teachers
who believed in me all those years ago
now here I am coming home

Bring out the yearbooks, bring out the photos
bring back the good times and laughter
now that I'm coming home.

Back in the Stands Again

Four years have come and gone
since that October night
when I first laid my eyes on you
you were sitting with my brothers and friends
we sure had fun those few games
now sometimes

I find myself back in the stands again
cheering on the football team
wishing it was 2004 again
but you're no longer around
though the magic I felt back then
still lingers in these Fall Skies

I still see a gleam in our eyes
when I look at the photo we took together
at the last game of the season
I'm glad fate allowed us to meet
you helped inspire some of these songs
now sometimes

I find myself back in the stands again
cheering on the football team
wishing it was 2004 again
but you're no longer around
though the magic I felt back then
still lingers in these Fall Skies.

October 29, 2004
Oak Hills vs. Elder

Chapter Three

See you in New Orleans

Hi Joe,

Having a great time.
the weather is beautiful.
We are so relaxed.
Talk to you on
Tuesday.
Love,
Sue + Dave

2008

Everybody Needs a Partner

Everybody needs a partner
to share in the jokes
Bud Abbott had Lou Costello
who's on first, what's on second
Lucy had Ethel to help her sneak
into Ricky's shows
Stewie has Brian
they are like Bob and Bing
always on the road to somewhere

Everybody needs a partner
to share in the glory
Joe Montana had Jerry Rice
Michael Jordan had Scottie Pippin
Randy Johnson had Curt Schilling
Babe Ruth had Lou Gehrig
they all won rings doing their thing

Everybody needs a partner
to help them through the hard times
Waylon had Jessi
Johnny had June
Ren had Stimpy
Shaggy has Scooby Doo
Charlie Brown has Snoopy

We all need a partner
to help pass the time
I'm glad you're with me tonight
you're my partner in crime
I wouldn't have it any other way
you always know what to say
when we find ourselves in trouble
everybody needs a partner.

My Mom, Cousin, Me, Dad, Sister-In-Law and brother

Me, Aunt Sue, my brother, and Uncle Dave

I Like to Dream

I like to dream
about mom's apple pie
and watching movies with my family
on Saturday nights

I like to dream
about lazy Sunday afternoons
having picnic by the river
with a bucket of chicken and sweet ice tea

I like to dream
about sunny days and tropical breezes
and the travels I've been on
sailing on the high seas

I like to dream
that my friends will drop in and say hi
I hope they turned out alright
in this crazy life.

Margaritas and Sunshine

Margaritas and sunshine
sharing a few rounds with my friends
as we sail the Gulf of Mexico
in my brand new boat
Kenny is tuning his guitar
Brandy is showing off her new boyfriend
we have until the sky turns purple and red
for a few more rounds of
margaritas and sunshine

I'm filling my cup of life
with cool tropical breezes
seashells and white sand
I'll fly the Jimmy Buffett flag with pride
as I eat steak and drink Tequila
by the light of the tiki candles
it won't be too much to handle
since I have

Margaritas and sunshine
sharing a few rounds with my friends
as we sail the Gulf of Mexico
in my brand new boat
Kenny is tuning his guitar
Brandy is showing off her new boyfriend
we have until the sky turns purple and red
for a few more rounds of
margaritas and sunshine.

My Piece of Heaven

Sea winds blow through the trees
hammocks swing in the breeze
I'm drinking a margarita deep freeze
the sun is shining high in the sky
I don't have a care in the world
not today at least
it's my day to rest

In my piece of Heaven
in my backyard
with a pool, my grill, my girls
where the sun always shines
I have all the time in the world
to do the things I love
in my piece of Heaven

I'm traveling to the Florida Keys
to hang out with the locals
share my adventures on the seas
and to show off my wife
see her there in the blue bikini
she can make a mean steak

In my piece of Heaven
in my backyard
with a pool, my grill, my girls
where the sun always shines
I have all the time in the world
to do the things I love
in my piece of Heaven.

I Need a Prayer Tonight

Rain rolls down glass of the fifth-floor windows
at Mercy Hospital
I can't believe the doctor's words
that you'd soon be leaving this world
I had to walk away and collect my thoughts
I sat down in the lounge and hung my head

I need a prayer tonight
I want to make everything right
and take away your suffering and pain
you don't deserve what you're going through
you were the kindest soul I ever met
I'm going to regret the things I didn't say
it's too hard to say goodbye
I need a prayer tonight

I walked back into your room
knowing the hour of the Lord would be here soon
I can feel the peace coming on
I need to be strong
when you finally let go
and head to the Promise Land
but until then

I need a prayer tonight
I want to make everything right
and take away your suffering and pain
you don't deserve what you're going through
you were the kindest soul I ever met
I'm going to regret the things I didn't say
it's too hard to say goodbye
I need a prayer tonight.

Grey Sky Morning

The hands of time are moving slow
the sun I haven't seen it's glow
these past few days
the blue skies I've come to known
have gone away

It's another grey sky morning
the rain is about to fall
fate made a bad call
when it took you out of my world forever
my heart broke in four
so at least one piece of me could be with you
you brought me the grey skies
when you told me goodbye

My wonderful world and it's bright colors
have faded to grey
I'm walking around in a haze
trying to figure out where I'm heading
since God brought you back to Heaven

It's another grey sky morning
the rain is about to fall
fate made a bad call
when it took you out of my world forever
my heart broke in four
so at least one piece of me could be with you
you brought me the grey skies
when you told me goodbye.

The Devil's Rain

I've seen rain falling on sunny days
I've heard thunder echo across the land
I've seen the dark clouds sneak up on the sun
made noon look like the dead of night
I've heard the wind whisper bad things
I've seen trees turn into twigs
and it's the Devil's rain that turns man away from God

I've seen it flood the Mighty Mississippi
batter the coast from Florida to Maine
I've seen it sweep away my friends
all we can do is pray
because when the demon's come to play
they bring the Devil's rain

I've seen it tempt man, turn their eyes red
I've seen hearts bled of their purity
I've seen the holiest of men brought down to their knees
begging for their souls to be saved
as they're being buried under flowers
being watered by the Devil's rain

I've seen rain falling on sunny days
I've heard thunder echo across the land
I've seen the dark clouds sneak up on the sun
made noon look like the dead of night
I've heard the wind whisper bad things
I've seen trees turn into twigs
and it's the Devil's rain that turns man away from God.

See you in New Orleans

Gone away is my dream
to walk Bourbon Street with you
God brought you home too soon
but the Cajun music still rings on Decatur Street
in my heart and soul, I know
I'll see you in New Orleans

I'm in a state of denial
as people remember your smile
down in Margaritaville
where we were supposed to chill
swapping stories with the locals
but there's only an empty seat
here in New Orleans

Condolences and cards hang on the walls
of all the bars
you were a shining star
now we remember your free spirit
no one can ever replace it
here in New Orleans

Gone away is my dream
to walk Bourbon Street with you
God brought you home too soon
but the Cajun music still rings on Decatur Street
in my heart and soul, I know
I'll see you in New Orleans.

My Aunt Sue and Me

Gypsy Rain

Gypsy rain fall on me tonight
I'm blue as blue as I can be
whiskey don't lift me up
like you do
it only brings me down
gypsy rain fall on me tonight

Gypsy rain you put a spell on me
hypnotizing me with every drop
I can't stop, it pulls me in
makes me act like a fool all night long
gypsy rain you put a spell on me

Gypsy rain knows my pain
as it travels on and on
not wanted anywhere
my tears flow with every passing cloud
gypsy rain knows my pain

Gypsy rain fall on me tonight
I'm blue as blue as I can be
whiskey don't lift me up
like you do
it only brings me down
gypsy rain fall on me tonight.

If Only

Time, what a concept
seems we rely on it too much
say haven't we seen it all

Boredom sets in over the summer
a blue moon rises over the trees
I have a feeling of Déjà vu by the bayou

I can see you standing next to me
but I can't see your reflection in the water
are you really here with me
or is the moonlight playing tricks on me

Memories spur the imagination
leads us to our destination
time will tell us when we're ready
to believe in the reality of our dreams

If only……
there was no such thing as pain
if only…..
there were no regrets
if only….
there was a way out of this nightmare
if only…
time could stand still
if only..
there was a new beginning
if only.
a lifetime wasn't cut short.

I can't Call Heaven

It's seven o' clock once again
wish I could call to tell you
what's been going on
the Reds won again
it's only Spring training
but a win is a win
I bought some posters you'd love to have seen
wish I could tell you these things

But I can't call Heaven
there's no direct line
wish I could hear your voice one more time
but the angels needed you home
you were gone before your time
wish I could call you at seven
but I can't call Heaven

I've seen the pennies you left me
I've seen you in my dreams
letting me know you're still near
though it's not the same
I know one day
we'll be together again
until then

I can't call Heaven
there's no direct line
wish I could hear your voice one more time
but the angels needed you home
you were gone before your time
wish I could call you at seven
but I can't call Heaven.

Lisa's Lullaby

You're a little angel in this world
touching people's lives
with your smile worth more than gold
you're the sunshine in the morning
the moon and stars at night
this is your song, your lullaby
so lay your head on your pillow
and let your dreams take you away

Seems like you knew your part
when I had a heavy heart
seems we needed each other's company
two weary souls on life's journey
who met at the right time
this is your song, your lullaby
so lay your head on your pillow
and let your dreams take you away

You're a little angel in this world
touching people's lives
with your smile worth more than gold
you're the sunshine in the morning
the moon and stars at night
this is your song, your lullaby
so lay your head on your pillow
and let your dreams take you away.

The Change

It was a hurricane
that wiped my world away
my future and dreams
were swept away by nature's fury
didn't have a clue what I was going to do
then you came along
my new horizon, and future
stood in

The change, like a brand-new year
starting over with a new hope and fire
it's the joy of standing on the beach
with your new bride hand in hand
watching the sunrises and sunsets
in this change of my life

I picked up my broken pieces
held them close to my heart
then placed them in my pocket
to remind me of who I was
and who you were
I'll carry on knowing
I can be strong, through

The change, like a brand-new year
starting over with a new hope and fire
it's the joy of standing on the beach
with your new bride hand in hand
watching the sunrises and sunsets
in this change of my life

We all get second chances
a miracle or two
when we see the light
and get touched by God's amazing grace
and receive a brand-new start in life.

Twilight of the Dawn

I see a new beginning
a picture being painted
with every word being said
between you and I
I hear a new song being played
with every shooting star in the sky

I thought my prayers went unheard
didn't think lightning would strike twice
but to my surprise
there you were in God's time

Now in the twilight of the dawn
I saw the light
too many times I've relied on signs
and not on my faith
I was lost, lost and lonely
Until I saw the twilight of the dawn

I see an eagle searching for its freedom
through a storm
reminding me of where I've been
now I'm back on the road to my destiny
and I owe it to

The twilight of the dawn
I saw the light
too many times I've relied on signs
and not on my faith
I was lost, lost and lonely
until I saw the twilight of the dawn

In the twilight of the dawn
lays our map, our destiny
hope and love endures the night
friendship is our greatest treasure
I finally found the truth
in the twilight of the dawn.

Goodbye 2008

Goodbye 2008, it wasn't all that great
I hope 2009 will allow the sun to shine
I've been to Hell and back a few times
I lost people who were close to me
the dream of life faded away
goodbye 2008, it wasn't all that great

It was a stormy year
with a million tears shed
over those who passed
I'll never forget the times we shared
for the memories will remain
goodbye 2008, it wasn't all that great

An angel came to me
to see me through the rain
though we're ages apart
we shared a common bond
that love will heal the pain
goodbye 2008, it wasn't all that great

Goodbye 2008, it wasn't all that great
I hope 2009 will allow the sun to shine
I've been to Hell and back a few times
I lost people who were close to me
the dream of life faded away
Goodbye 2008, it wasn't all that great.

Epilogue

In 2015 my Uncle Dave passed away. He was married to my Aunt Sue who passed away in 2008. I wrote a song about them, and who they were.

They were both free spirits, and loved going to concerts, football games, baseball games, loved collecting posters and pins of different events. You could find them in Chicago and New Orleans at different musical festivals.

After they passed I got a few of their mementos and it was like a map of their life of where they been.

Dave and Sue

Who They Were

They were soul mates, both free spirits
you could run into them in New Orleans, Chicago
at the local and national jazz festivals
going backstage to meet the singers
they cheered for the Bengals and Saints
always wore smiles and made friends wherever they went

They collected bobbleheads,tailgated before the big games
drank at the bars during Mardi Gras
bought pins and posters as mementos
to remember the moments they shared
they sat in the best seats in the house
and were the life of the party always
having a good time

I made sure to call them every week
to talk about the Reds or upcoming concerts
didn't want to miss out on a big event
I'm a free spirit, I take after them
having good times, capturing the moments
living it up, making bets at festivals
winning and losing money all in fun

Now I have some of their mementos of the places they've been
it helps me understand, who they really were
and what meant most to them
they were soul mates, free spirits
always having a good time
and wearing smiles wherever they went.

Dave and Sue

Copyright